CAREERS THAT SAVE LIVES

FIREFIGHTER

Louise Spilsbury

W

FRANKLIN WATTS
LONDON • SYDNEY

Franklin Watts
First published in Great Britain in 2016 by The Watts Publishing Group

Credits
Series Editors: Sarah Eason and Jennifer Sanderson
Series Designer: Emma DeBanks

Photo credits: Cover: Shutterstock: Fluke Samed (top), Digital Storm (bottom);
Inside: Dreamstime: Martin Brayley 9, 10, 17, 23, 28, Nomadsoul1 24–25;
Shutterstock: Baloncici 16, Marilyn Barbone 11t, Tatiana Belova 6t, Denisenko
8, 12, 16, 22, 30, 32, Digital Storm 11, EDG 22–23, Sarah Jessup 19 b, John
Kasawa 1, 26, Koka55 15, Patricia Marks 27, Monkey Business Images 12, 24, NF
Photography 18–19, Anton Oparin 21, Valentina Petrov 20, Phichai 2, Phiseksit 6,
8, 10, 14, 17, 18, 21, Photovova 4, Potowizard 7, T-Design 27, Worradirek 14.

Dewey number: 363.3'78
ISBN: 978 1 4451 4505 1

Printed in China

FSC
www.fsc.org
MIX
Paper from
responsible sources
FSC® C104740

Franklin Watts
An imprint of
Hachette Children's Group
Part of The Watts Publishing Group
Carmelite House
50 Victoria Embankment
London EC4Y 0DZ

An Hachette UK Company
www.hachette.co.uk

www.franklinwatts.co.uk

CONTENTS

MAKING A DIFFERENCE

Police officer, lifeguard and firefighter, these are all careers that count. Careers such as these are special because they make a huge difference in other people's lives. Some people look for a job with a big **salary**, but this will not necessarily make them happy. Studies show that careers that make people happiest are the ones in which workers help others, are creative or use their knowledge and skills. Workers who do not have any challenges, do not use their skills or knowledge or do the same thing day after day may often feel bored at work or not enjoy the work they do.

While most people run in the opposite direction of a fire, it is a firefighter's job to face the smoke and flames to rescue anyone trapped by the blaze.

Take the Challenge

If you choose to work in a career that helps others, you will face challenges and difficulties. However, no two days will be the same and you will feel a huge sense of satisfaction when you make a difference in other people's lives. Some people work to improve people's health, help them during difficult times or teach them new skills. In this book, we will look at the work of firefighters – heroes who save lives and property.

A Career for You?

Here are three things you can do to work out if a career that counts might be right for you:

- Get to know yourself. What are your strengths, values, interests and **ambitions**?
- Find out as much as you can about your chosen job and what it is really like. Reading this book is a good place to start.
- Talk to your teachers and a **career advisor**. They might suggest options that you did not know about.

HEROES WHO SAVE LIVES

Being a firefighter is one of the toughest jobs a person can do. A firefighter is trained to save the lives of people in danger, which often means putting his or her own life on the line. A firefighter helps people in many different and dangerous situations, such as rescuing people from burning buildings and helping those trapped in vehicles at road accidents. On call both day and night, being a firefighter is a job that requires true commitment and courage.

Firefighters are trained to work out how dangerous a situation is and if they can safely attempt a rescue.

WHAT MAKES A GREAT FIREFIGHTER?

Firefighters follow a long and **rigorous** training programme to make sure they are able to safely carry out their role. However, there are also some important **characteristics** all firefighters need in order to be able to do this dangerous job. Firefighters must be:
- Trustworthy: their team and the public depend on them.
- Able to listen: firefighters must follow instructions.
- Brave: firefighters put the needs of others first.

Which of the above do you think is most important and why?

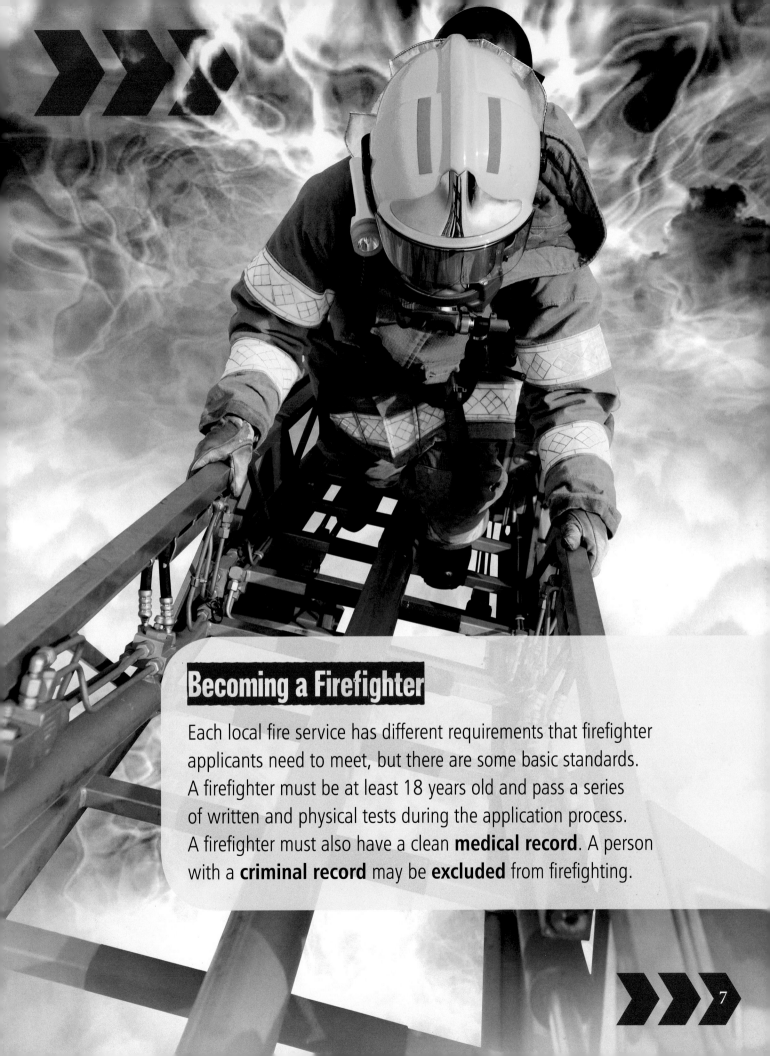

Becoming a Firefighter

Each local fire service has different requirements that firefighter applicants need to meet, but there are some basic standards. A firefighter must be at least 18 years old and pass a series of written and physical tests during the application process. A firefighter must also have a clean **medical record**. A person with a **criminal record** may be **excluded** from firefighting.

A TYPICAL DAY

No two days are the same for firefighters. Firefighters do not even work regular hours. Some work 48-hour shifts at a time and each shift brings new challenges. This is what one 24-hour shift might be like, if there were no emergency calls.

A FIREFIGHTER'S DAY

- **8 am** Firefighters line up for **roll call** and to get their schedule for the day, which will include the duties and training they will have between calls.
- **8:15 am** The first job is checking, repairing and cleaning all the equipment.
- **9:30 am** Firefighters live in the fire station for long stretches of time, so in the mornings they clean their living quarters, too.
- **10 am** Work out! Firefighters must be fit and strong, so they try to spend some time in the gym every day.
- **11 am** Before lunch, firefighters do jobs such as collecting food and other supplies.
- **1 pm** After lunch, firefighters take part in activities that include training, **fire-safety inspections**, public education sessions and station tours.
- **6 pm** After dinner and until bedtime, many of the firefighters on duty complete reports on fire or emergency **incidents**, work on special projects or study for tests.

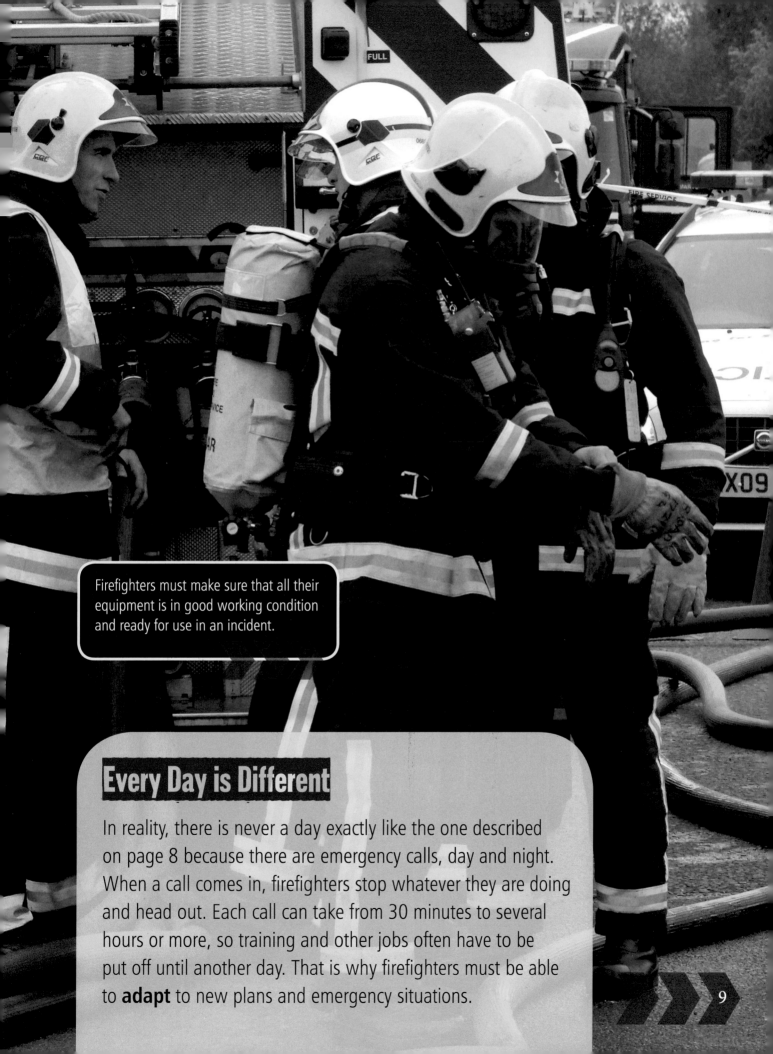

Firefighters must make sure that all their equipment is in good working condition and ready for use in an incident.

Every Day is Different

In reality, there is never a day exactly like the one described on page 8 because there are emergency calls, day and night. When a call comes in, firefighters stop whatever they are doing and head out. Each call can take from 30 minutes to several hours or more, so training and other jobs often have to be put off until another day. That is why firefighters must be able to **adapt** to new plans and emergency situations.

EQUIPMENT

The one job that must be done every day without fail, no matter how many calls there are, is checking the equipment. Firefighting equipment must be working properly at all times. How well it works could be the difference between life and death.

Fire engines are large trucks that can carry firefighting crews, equipment and water to the scene of an emergency. Crew members ride in the cab at the front and tools are kept in lockers on the sides. On the back is a turntable ladder that can turn in all directions. It also has sections that can extend to reach tall buildings.

Firefighters rely on equipment such as long hoses to get the job done, and to keep safe.

WHAT MAKES A GREAT FIREFIGHTER?

Firefighters work with a lot of technology, including thermal imaging cameras, sometimes called **thermal imagers**, **satellite** maps, computers and other digital equipment. The equipment helps firefighters predict wind directions and access information needed to **monitor** and fight a fire. Do you think understanding how the equipment works is as important as being fit enough to fight fires?

helmet

mask

torch

protective suit

thermal imaging camera

axe

Among the axes, hoses, **fire extinguishers** and other equipment on board a fire engine, firefighters also have **oxygen** tanks and thermal imaging cameras. Burning buildings are filled with smoke and poisonous gases that make it hard to see and can choke people. Firefighters wear masks to protect their faces. They also carry a tank of clean air that they breathe in through a tube fitted to the mask. Firefighters use thermal imaging cameras to see through smoke and darkness so they can search for victims trapped in fires.

ALL SYSTEMS GO!

When an emergency happens, an alarm sounds in the fire station and the details and location of the incident flash up on a computer screen. Then, it is all systems go for the firefighters!

Firefighters change into their uniforms within seconds. Uniforms are stored hanging up so firefighters can put them on quickly. The uniform is vital for safety. It has:

- Fasteners made of Velcro, which are easy to close.
- A tough, plastic helmet to protect the head.
- A thick waterproof and fireproof jacket covered in **reflective** strips.
- Thick waterproof and fireproof boots with steel toe caps to protect feet from falling **debris**. The boots also have solid soles in case firefighters step on something sharp.

In the fire engine, a map flashes up on a screen for the driver to follow. Another crew member stays on the radio for updates from the station. The fire engine needs to move quickly, so its noisy siren warns other drivers to get out of the way. As the fire engine speeds through the streets, the firefighters prepare themselves for what they might find at the scene.

Firefighters race to their engines and speed through the streets to get to the scene of a fire quickly.

Knowing the Local Area

Firefighters have to take time to get to know local streets and buildings around their fire station. This is so that they can respond to emergency calls **efficiently**.

13

FIGHTING FIRES

Every fire is unique and firefighters have to fight different fires in different ways. However, one rule remains the same whatever the fire. Firefighters must deprive the fire of one of the three things it needs: **fuel**, oxygen or heat.

Firefighters use hoses from a water tank or from a street **hydrant** to spray cold water onto the fire. Hoses have pumps that can spray water 91 metres away or more. It can take several firefighters to hold a hose because it sprays water with such force. Firefighters remove fuel, wood and other **flammable** materials in a building by spraying foam or powder to stop oxygen spreading. They also use axes to remove walls and roofs. Firefighters may stand on a platform at the top of the ladder to spray roofs or to reach people trapped in tall buildings.

firefighters holding a hose

WHAT MAKES A GREAT FIREFIGHTER?

Firefighters need to be practical, and they also need to be able to know how fires work. They study the science of fires to understand them better. How do you think this knowledge might help them respond better to fires?

Firefighting Roles

At the scene of a fire, firefighters work under a commanding officer and have specific jobs to do. Hose operators connect the hoses to fire hydrants and aim the water towards the fire. The pump operators control the water flow. Other firefighters guide the extended ladders or enter burning buildings to rescue victims.

Firefighters work in teams. The firefighter at the top of a ladder relies on another crew member in the fire engine to control where the ladder goes.

CRASH RESCUE

Fighting fires is only about 20 per cent of what a firefighter does. Firefighters also answer requests to attend other emergencies, such as traffic accidents. Firefighters go to traffic accidents because there are often fires at the scene or injured people trapped in vehicles.

As soon as firefighters arrive at a crash site, they check for safety. First, they make sure that vehicles are not on fire or leaking dangerous fluids. Then, they put up warnings to keep other drivers clear of the area. To rescue someone trapped in a vehicle as quickly as possible, they explain to the victim what is happening and use a **tarpaulin** to protect him or her from debris. The firefighters may use a wide variety of hand tools and mechanical equipment, such as **hydraulic spreaders** and cutters, special saws, winches and rams to safely break open a vehicle.

firefighter's axe

Fit to Fight Fires

Firefighters often have to move heavy objects, operate heavy equipment and carry victims from damaged vehicles or burning buildings while wearing bulky safety gear. Being in top physical shape is absolutely essential for those following a career in firefighting.

WHAT MAKES A GREAT FIREFIGHTER?

Sometimes firefighters are the first at an emergency scene, such as a car accident in which there are **multiple fatalities**. Facing situations like these can be emotionally challenging. How do you think firefighters prepare themselves to cope with some of the distressing duties they are asked to perform?

Firefighters use powerful tools like these to cut through metal and release victims trapped in cars and other vehicles.

FOREST FIREFIGHTERS

Forest fires and other wildfires are very dangerous. Winds can make a fire spread quickly and change direction without warning. Forest fires can also go on for days or weeks, so firefighters may work without time off for long periods. Being a forest firefighter is tough and challenging, and it can sometimes be a frightening job.

Helicopters are used to deliver firefighters and their equipment to forest fires and to drop water over areas of fire.

WHAT MAKES A GREAT FIREFIGHTER?

Firefighters use a variety of tools, both hand tools and power tools. It is important to be able to understand how these work and how to use them. How do you think these tools could help firefighters deal with emergency situations, such as car accidents or burning buildings?

Forest firefighters tackle fires in different ways. Their main technique is to use bulldozers and other equipment to cut down trees and dig up plants to clear a ring around the fire. When the fire reaches this area, it can no longer spread because there is no fuel in its path. Sometimes, firefighters carry out a controlled burn of all the fuel between the fire and a boundary, such as a road or stream, to stop the fire. Firefighters also fly special aircraft over the fire and drop water, **fire retardant** and chemicals (foam) on the fire to put it out.

smoke jumper

Smoke Jumpers

Some forest firefighters are known as smoke jumpers. Smoke jumpers are trained to parachute from aeroplanes into remote areas where a wildfire has started. They try to control the fire and stop it spreading. Firefighting tools, food and water are dropped by parachute to the smoke jumpers after they land.

DISASTER!

Firefighters are also called out to help after bomb incidents, hurricanes, floods or other disasters. These calls are especially challenging as firefighters often have to think of new ways to tackle such emergencies.

Hazmat suits cover a firefighter's whole body to protect him or her from hazardous materials.

Controlling Danger

Some firefighters work in **hazardous materials units**. They are specially trained to control and clean up dangerous materials at oil spills and chemical accidents. By doing so, they protect citizens from exposure to hazardous substances. They wear special hazmat suits and use equipment to identify different and dangerous substances.

In a disaster situation, there may be injured people trapped in burning houses, collapsed roads and buildings and hazardous waters. Cables and pipes may be damaged, leaving the area without power and with the danger of more explosions or shocks. Firefighters work as part of a **task force**, alongside other rescue services and engineers, medics and other specialists. They put out fires, rescue people, move large debris to make way for rescues and inspect sites for dangers, such as gas leaks. They also help clean up and check sites after dealing with the incident.

WHAT MAKES A GREAT FIREFIGHTER?

At the scene of a disaster, a lot can be happening at once. Firefighters need to co-operate and get along with a wide range of people, both from in their own crews and people from other emergency services. Their lives and the lives of other people depend on it. What other qualities do you think firefighters need to be good team players?

Firefighters help people in different kinds of emergencies, including earthquakes and hurricanes.

MEDICAL AID

As part of helping to protect people and places, firefighters may also have the responsibility of providing emergency medical care at the site of an incident. They are often first to arrive at a scene, and knowing how to treat injured victims immediately saves countless lives.

A large number of a fire department's emergency responses are calls for medical aid, for things such as accidents at home and work or injuries resulting from traffic accidents. Firefighters are trained to give first aid, such as bandaging wounds. Some specially trained firefighters can also treat patients for life-threatening injuries or illnesses. For example, they will give **CPR** to someone who is not breathing properly or is suffering a heart attack.

People involved in crash scenes may be badly injured. Firefighters must be prepared to give emergency medical treatment to people until full medical help arrives.

Qualified to Save Lives

Many fire brigades also train some of their firefighters to become trauma technicians. This training gives those firefighters the skills they need to be able to treat people who have life-threatening injuries, to keep them alive until ambulance services arrive.

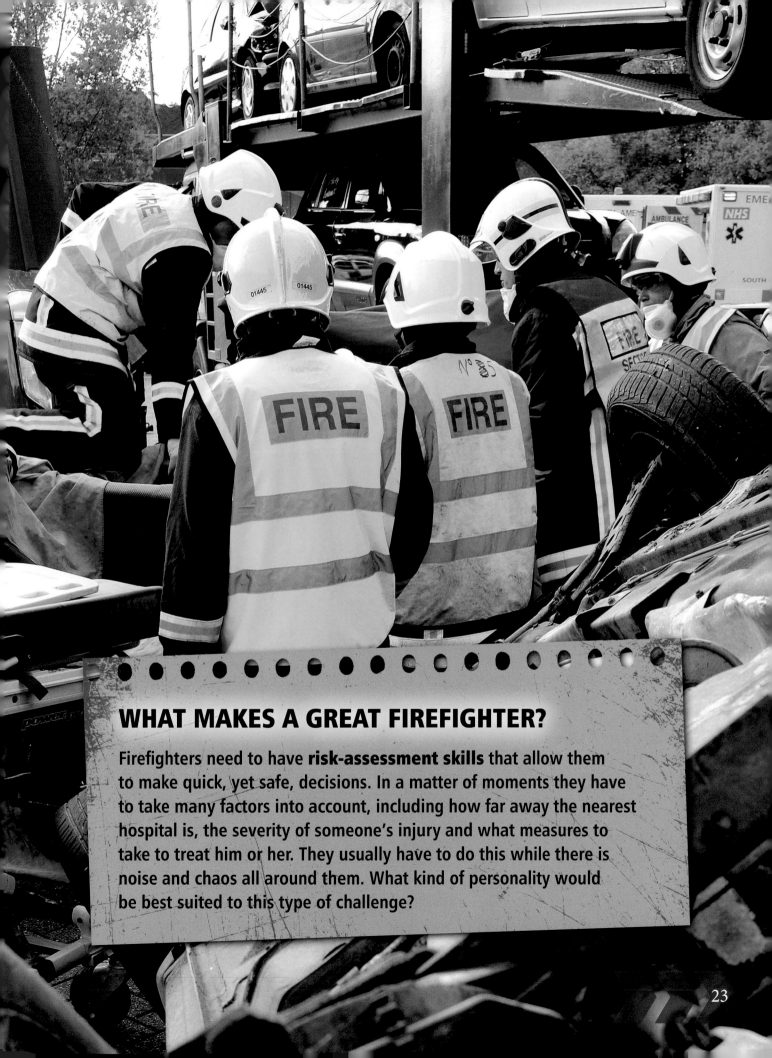

WHAT MAKES A GREAT FIREFIGHTER?

Firefighters need to have **risk-assessment skills** that allow them to make quick, yet safe, decisions. In a matter of moments they have to take many factors into account, including how far away the nearest hospital is, the severity of someone's injury and what measures to take to treat him or her. They usually have to do this while there is noise and chaos all around them. What kind of personality would be best suited to this type of challenge?

SAFETY FIRST

Another important job that firefighters do is to work with the local community to increase people's level of fire-safety awareness. This helps prevent fires and accidents occurring in the first place.

WHAT MAKES A GREAT FIREFIGHTER?

Firefighters need to be able to engage with all groups within the community, but especially with those at risk, such as the elderly and children. Clear **communication** is vital. Why do you think firefighters must be able to listen to what others are saying and explain information clearly?

Firefighters educate the public in different ways. They visit schools and community centres to give talks and presentations about what to do if there is a fire. They explain how people should get out of a burning building, stay out and call the emergency number. They talk to people about safety at home and the importance of smoke alarms. Firefighters talk about fire safety and enforce fire-safety standards in public areas and business places. For example, they advise people about alarms and sprinkler systems and check that safety features, such as fire escapes, work well.

Investigating Fires

Some firefighters become fire investigators. They find where the fire started and they look for evidence if **arson** is suspected. They work out how a fire began and they may have to testify in court if, for example, a fire happened because a company did not follow fire-safety rules.

Firefighters stress the importance of fitting smoke detectors and making sure that they are working correctly.

RISKS AND REWARDS

Firefighting is a tough business. In fact, it is one of the most challenging and dangerous jobs in the world. So, why do firefighters do it?

Firefighters are constantly rushing into unknown situations in which they might be injured or killed. They often face dangers that include collapsing floors and walls, traffic accidents and exposure to smoke and flames. However, firefighters are highly trained and they work with excellent safety equipment, which lessens the risks of the job. Firefighters are confident in their training and want to do what they can to help. Their reward is the feeling of satisfaction and accomplishment that comes from saving someone's life or property.

Always Learning

Firefighters never stop learning and training. Attending lectures, doing practice drills and following other training courses are an important part of the job. Training takes place throughout a firefighter's career. Firefighters need to master many skills and need to keep updating and adding to them.

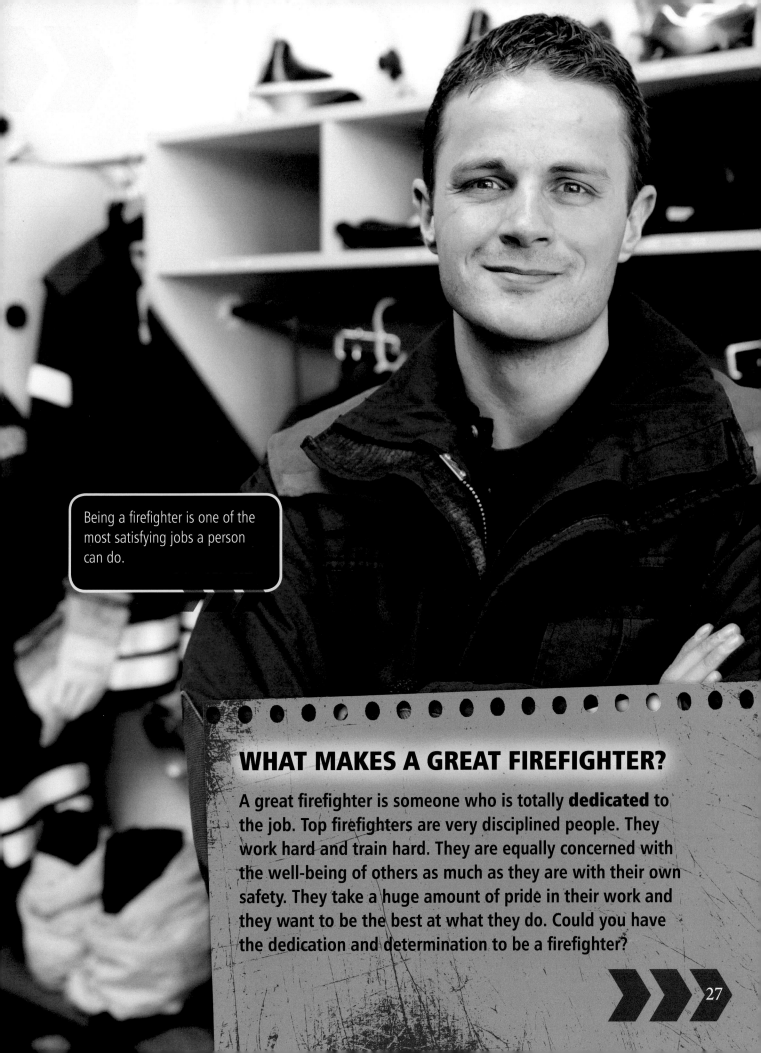

Being a firefighter is one of the most satisfying jobs a person can do.

WHAT MAKES A GREAT FIREFIGHTER?

A great firefighter is someone who is totally **dedicated** to the job. Top firefighters are very disciplined people. They work hard and train hard. They are equally concerned with the well-being of others as much as they are with their own safety. They take a huge amount of pride in their work and they want to be the best at what they do. Could you have the dedication and determination to be a firefighter?

COULD YOU HAVE A CAREER AS A FIREFIGHTER?

Do you want to become a firefighter? Following these steps will help you reach your goal.

Subjects to study at school **You do not need to study particular subjects but maths, science, engineering and technology will be useful. Take opportunities to practice teamwork while at school, and to mix and deal with people from a wide range of backgrounds.**

Work experience **If you are 16 years of age or older, it may be possible to do work experience at your local fire station in an observer capacity. You will have to write to the fire and rescue service directly,**

Exams to pass You do not need particular qualifications to become a firefighter because firefighters mainly train on the job, although they might help you stand out from the competition during the selection process.

University You do not need a university degree, but some universities offer a fire service pre-recruitment course. If you are interested, a degree in fire science, fire technology or a subject such as maths, chemistry or biology can improve your chances of getting a job and getting promoted.

Life experience Get fit and stay fit. Firefighters have to be physically fit and have to pass a medical examination before they will be accepted.

Improve your CV Volunteer in your community. Do not volunteer just to increase your chances of getting a job but because you have a real interest in caring for your fellow citizens. You do not have to do something fire-related, just show that you want to care for people in your community.

Getting the job Applicants are expected to pass written, physical and medical examinations prior to being considered for a job. Once you have been employed, you will do physical training exercises and first aid training.

GLOSSARY

adapt To change in order to cope with a new situation.

ambitions Hopes and goals.

aptitude A natural ability to do something.

arson The criminal act of deliberately setting fire to property.

career advisor A person trained to help people find out which career is best for them.

characteristics Features or qualities belonging to a particular person or thing.

communication The giving and receiving of information.

CPR An acronym for cardiopulmonary resuscitation. CPR is a first aid technique that can be used if someone is not breathing properly or if his or her heart has stopped.

criminal record A record of the crimes a person has committed.

debris The bits and pieces scattered at the scene of an accident or other incident.

dedicated Devoted and committed to something.

efficiently To do something well and quickly.

excluded Not allowed to take part.

fire extinguishers Portable devices that discharge a jet of water, foam, gas or other material to put out a fire.

fire-safety inspections Checks carried out to be sure an area is not at risk of fire.

fire retardant A substance that makes fuels less likely to catch fire or slows down how quickly they catch fire.

flammable Easily set on fire.

fuel A substance that creates heat when it is burned.

hazardous materials units Teams that are trained to deal with dangerous substances.

hazmat suits Rubber and plastic coverings that protect people from harmful chemicals and other hazardous substances.

hydrant A water pipe, usually in a street, with a nozzle to which a fire hose can be attached.

hydraulic spreaders Tools used by emergency rescue workers to break open vehicles or other spaces where people are trapped.

incidents Accidents or dangerous events.

medical record A record of all the health care a person has received.

monitor To check and watch something closely.

multiple fatalities Many deaths.

oxygen A gas found in the air.

reflective A surface that light or heat bounces off.

rigorous Extremely thorough.

risk-assessment skills Skills that enable people to decide how dangerous a situation is.

roll call The process of calling out a list of names to establish who is present.

salary A fixed regular payment, typically paid on a monthly basis.

satellite A machine that orbits around the Earth. It collects, receives and passes on information.

tarpaulin A plastic covering.

task force A group given a specific task or job to do.

thermal imagers Devices that help people see in the dark.

FURTHER READING

Career As A Firefighter: What They Do, How to Become One, and What the Future Holds! Brian Rogers, CreateSpace Independent Publishing Platform

Diary of a Firefighter
Angela Royston, Capstone Publishing

Firefighter (Here to Help)
Rachel Blount, Franklin Watts

Fire Service (Emergency 999)
Kathryn Walker, Wayland Books

WEBSITES

Find out more about what firefighters do at:
www.fireserviceinfo.com/firefighter.html

Learn what it takes to be a firefighter at:
https://nationalcareersservice.direct.gov.uk/advice/planning/jobprofiles/Pages/firefighter.aspx

Discover how firefighter training works at:
www.fireservice.co.uk

Learn more about fire safety at:
www.firefacts.org

Find out how to keep your home safe from fire with these games and activities:
www.london-fire.gov.uk/GamesAndActivities.asp

Note to parents and teachers
Every effort has been made by the Publisher to ensure that these websites contain no inappropriate or offensive material. However, because of the nature of the Internet, it is impossible to guarantee that the contents of these sites will not be altered. We strongly advise that Internet access is supervised by a responsible adult.

INDEX